This is a book that's made for you,
With things to read, and see and do –
To count, or find or figure out –
To match or solve or think about.

There are nursery rhymes you already know,
But once they get started, off they go!
They turn into puzzles and games and fun
With pictures to help you enjoy each one.

Perhaps you'll share some games with your brother
Or sister or aunt, or father or mother,
And when you've done them all the way through,
Just start again and you'll find something new!

The last few lines of every rhyme
Explain the puzzle every time,
And tell you how you can join right in,
So turn the page – it's time to begin!

Books from OWL are published in Canada by
Greey de Pencier Books,
56 The Esplanade, Suite 306,
Toronto, Ontario M5E 1A7

This book was published with the generous support of the
Canada Council and the Ontario Arts Council.

Canadian Cataloguing in Publication Data

Patterson, Pat.
Hickory Dickory Duck, A Book of Funny Mixed-Up Rhymes and Picture Puzzles

ISBN 0-919872-72-7

1. Picture puzzles – Juvenile literature. 2. Nursery rhymes.
I. Weissmann, Joe, 1947- II. Title.

GV1507.P47P37 j793.73 C81-094935-0

Printed in Hong Kong

Designed by Julie Colantonio

1 2 3 4 5 95 94 93 92 91 90

Hickory Dickory Duck

A Book of Funny Mixed-Up Nursery Rhymes And Picture Puzzles

Written by Pat Patterson

Illustrated by Joe Weissmann

OWL

GREEY DE PENCIER BOOKS

THE QUEEN OF HEARTS

The Queen of Hearts,
She made some tarts
All on a summer's day;
The Knave of Hearts,
He stole the tarts
And took them all away.

The Knave of Hearts
He hid the tarts
So no one else could eat.
"Tonight," he said,
"While the folks are in bed,
I'll have a tasty treat!"

The King of Hearts
Was crazy for tarts,
So he searched the whole night through.
By morning sun
He'd found just one.
The rest is up to you!

A dozen tarts
All shaped like hearts
Are hidden for you to spy.
Where can they be?
Just look and see!
You'll find them if you try.

G. Weinmann

Three Little Kittens

Three little kittens
Lost their mittens
And they began to cry.
"Oh Mom and Dad
Will be so mad,
We won't get any pie!"

Their parents were cross
When they heard of the loss,
And they said, "Those mittens were made
In colours to go
With your ties, you know,
So look for the very same shade."

The kittens went looking
While Father was cooking.
"No mittens, no pie," Mother said.
They checked all the chairs,
The tables, the stairs,
The cupboard, the dresser, the bed.

Now use *your* eyes
And look at the ties;
Their colour will give you a clue.
Can you find two mittens
For each of the kittens?
Let's see how well you can do.

MARY MARY, QUITE CONTRARY

Mary Mary, quite contrary,
How does your garden grow?
"With silver bells and cockleshells
And pretty maids all in a row."

"I've blue tomatoes and pink potatoes,
Navy blue lettuce and peas;
With orange beans and purple greens,
I grow things as I please."

"My pears are plummy, my plums are crummy,
My peaches and apples are square.
I've polka-dot berries and big checkered cherries
And parsnips that grow in the air."

"You'll have to pardon the fact that my garden
Is quite the weirdest in town.
But concentrate and you'll find eight
Things that are upside down!"

THERE WAS AN OLD WOMAN

There was an Old Woman
Who lived in a shoe,
She had so many children
She didn't know what to do.

And when it came to bedtime,
She couldn't find the beds.
The children slept in lampshades
Or standing on their heads.

While some were in pyjamas
And others wore their kilts,
A few put on their slippers
And some walked 'round on stilts.

They washed in peanut butter
And brushed their teeth with glue.
Now, see how many children
You find inside that shoe.

HEY DIDDLE DIDDLE

Hey diddle diddle,
The cat and the fiddle,
The cow jumped over the moon.
The little dog laughed
To see such sport
And the dish ran away with the spoon.

Hey daddle daddle,
A fish with a saddle,
A horse ran over the sea.
A shark and a pig
Were dancing a jig
While a fisherman landed a flea.

Hey duddle duddle,
A ship sailed a puddle,
A dragon was wearing a dress.
Now, find some swings
And other things
That start with the letter "S."

Little Boy Blue

Little Boy Blue, come blow your horn.
The sheep's in the meadow,
the cow's in the corn.
Where is the boy who looks after the sheep?
He's under the haystack, fast asleep.

Little Boy Blue, come ring your bell.
The cat's on the kennel, the dog's in the well.
The pig and the pony have gone in the house.
A worm and a snail are chasing a mouse.

Little Boy Blue, come blow your whistle.
A spider is singing while eating a thistle.
A horse in the hen-house is scrambling eggs.
A centipede's sitting there counting its legs.

Little Boy Blue, look left, look right.
One way is day, the other night.
Things are the same, and yet they're not.
How many differences can you spot?

SING A SONG OF SIXPENCE

Sing a song of sixpence,
A pocket full of rye;
Four and twenty blackbirds
Baked in a pie.

When the pie was opened,
The blackbirds flew away,
"Sorry, folks!" they sweetly sang,
"You can't eat us today!"

The King, he dressed for jogging
And gave the birds a chase.
He tripped upon a turtledove
And fell upon his face.

The birds all chirped and chuckled,
Then hastily they hid.
Do you think you can find them all?
The poor King never did!

LITTLE BO-PEEP

Little Bo-peep has lost her sheep
And can't tell where to find them.
Leave them alone and they'll come home,
Bringing their tails behind them.

Poor Bo-peep began to weep
As still her sheep were straying.
But when she rose and blew her nose,
She found them gaily playing.

"Good grief!" said she. "What's this I see?
Your tails you have forgotten!
What shall I do with all of you?
You really do look rotten!"

To help Bo-peep, please take each sheep
And find the tail that matches it.
The colour will be the same, you see,
Just right when she attaches it.

OLD KING COLE

Old King Cole was a merry old soul,
And a merry old soul was he;
He called for his pipe and he called for his bowl
And he called for his fiddlers three.

The fiddlers brought their fiddles and bows,
But before they could start to play,
A beaver who blew on a garden hose
Had begun to swing and sway.

Then through the window flew some flutes,
While trumpeters came by the door,
And a tot with a tuba gave two toots
As he squeezed through a crack in the floor.

And still more came, 'til the King cried, "Hey!
That's too much noise for me!"
Now, you count the players who came to play
Along with the fiddlers three.

OLD MOTHER HUBBARD

Old Mother Hubbard,
She went to the cupboard
To get her poor dog a bone;
But when she got there
The cupboard was bare
And so the poor dog had none.

She did all her mopping
And then she went shopping
And brought home a couple of tonnes
Of hamburger, ham
And lemons and lamb
And bacon, bananas and buns.

Ms. Hubbard bought oodles
Of nibbles and noodles
And peanuts and pickles and prunes,
Two pink ice cream cones,
A bundle of bones,
And fishcakes and fat macaroons.

Now look in the cupboard
Of old Mother Hubbard,
Don't miss each package and tin,
Then just give a shout
When you think you've found out
The things she didn't put in.

Noodles
Nibbles
LAMB
HAMBURGER
Macaroons
PRUNES

LITTLE MISS MUFFET

Little Miss Muffet
Sat on a tuffet,
Eating her curds and whey.
Along came a spider
And sat down beside her
And frightened Miss Muffet away.

"Oh, why must I run so?
I shouldn't have done so."
Miss Muffet was cross as could be.
"It's not all that scary,
It's just rather hairy.
I think I'll invite it to tea."

She got so excited,
She also invited
A lot of small creatures she knew.
They hungrily hurried;
Some slithered, some scurried,
Some hopped and some crawled and some flew.

The friends of Miss Muffet
Sat all 'round the tuffet
And some flew right up in the tree.
Now can you be clever
Or quick or whatever
And name all the creatures you see?

HICKORY DICKORY DOCK

Hickory dickory dock,
The mouse ran up the clock.
The clock struck one,
The mouse ran down.
Hickory dickory dock.

Hickory dickory duck,
Again the clock has struck.
The duck and mouse
Ran round the house.
Hickory dickory duck.

Hickory dickory dack,
The duck began to quack.
She shook her leg
And laid an egg.
Hickory dickory dack.

Hickory dickory dong,
Do you see anything wrong?
Are some things here
A little queer?
Or do they not belong?

CLUES AND ANSWERS

THE QUEEN OF HEARTS: Look high, look low to find all twelve tarts. But don't count the one the King has already found.

THREE LITTLE KITTENS: Look for the missing mittens in the toy box and the cookie jar, on the chandelier and the chicken's head, under Father cat's foot and with the mice.

MARY MARY QUITE CONTRARY: The watering can, the basket, the rabbit, the dog, the bird, a parsnip, a cloud, and a tree are all upside down.

THERE WAS AN OLD WOMAN: Twenty children are crowded upstairs and downstairs inside the shoe. One is outside.

HEY DIDDLE DIDDLE: There are at least 24 things beginning with "s" including stars, snow, swings, skunk, socks, skates, scarf, snail, shell, squirrels, spaghetti, spoon, strawberries, shark, suspenders, ship, sails, smoke stack, smoke, saddle, shoes, spots on cow, stripes on pig's pants and smiles all around. If you try hard, you may even find more.

LITTLE BOY BLUE: There are 14 differences in the two pictures. Most people miss the open door and the extra window on the house. Did you spot them?

SING A SONG OF SIXPENCE: Did you find all 24 birds? There's even one hiding behind the teddy bear.

LITTLE BO-PEEP: Did you find all eight bows? Don't miss the purple one hidden in the flowers.

OLD KING COLE: There are 23 musicians. The hardest to find is the horn player coming through the door. Did you count him?

OLD MOTHER HUBBARD: The bag of bones is missing, of course. But Old Mother Hubbard hasn't put the ice cream cones away either.

LITTLE MISS MUFFET: Look for a turtle, a frog, a worm, a grasshopper, a beetle, three rabbits, a duck, a snail, a ladybug, three mice, a spider, a squirrel, a butterfly, a fox, a goat, a bluebird, a snake, an owl and a blackbird. What a party!

HICKORY DICKORY DOCK: Look carefully at the light, the picture of the duck, the fishbowl, the piano, the stove, the cat, the chair, the pig, the dog, the fire engine and the sailboat. Something's queer about all of these.